There's an Alien in my Spaghetti

Written by Kay Woodward

Illustrated by Ilaria Campana

Collins

1 The day it all began

Zoha was slurping spaghetti on the day it all began.

The sunlight vanished. It became darker than night. The wind roared like a head teacher in a very bad mood.

"How odd!" Dad shouted. "The weather forecaster said there'd be blue skies and a light breeze, not *this*."

"I can't see a thing!" wailed Mum.

Zap! There was a blinding flash of lightning that lit up the kitchen.

Smash! The window burst open.

Whoosh! Wind rushed into the room.

Boom! The thunder was so loud that it made Zoha's ears sing.

Thud! The window blew shut again.

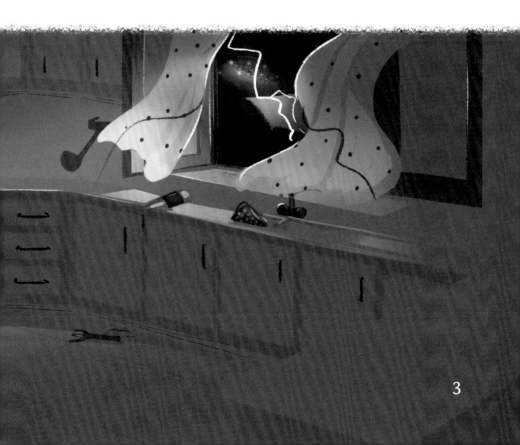

Everything was still.

It was as if the storm had
never happened. The sun came
out and the wind stopped roaring.

Zoha had the feeling that something
astonishing had just happened.
But what? She stuck her fork
into her bowl again. Then she froze.
Something was hiding in a tangle
of spaghetti. It was small and oval
and very, very shiny.

"Wow ..." Zoha breathed.

"Wow!" said Mum and Dad.
But they weren't talking about
the shiny something. They were
gazing at the blue sky outside.

So Zoha quickly stuck her fingers
into the squelchy spaghetti and
pulled out ...

... a tiny, silver spaceship.

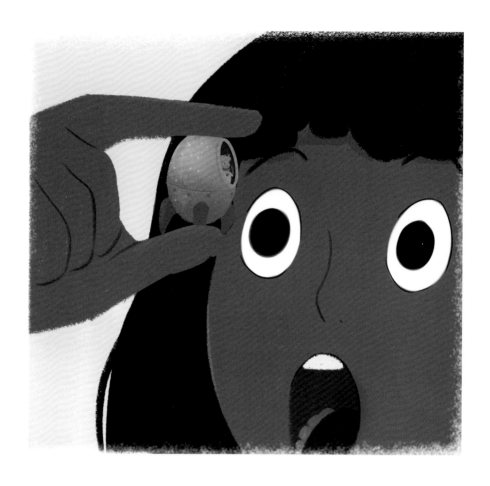

There was a tiny window in the tiny spaceship and
Zoha looked inside. A tiny alien looked back at her.

"Eeek!" Zoha squeaked.

The alien put a finger to his lips and said, "Shhh."
His voice was so quiet that Zoha had to lean forward
to hear him.

"What is it, dear?" said Mum.

"Are you OK?" asked Dad.

"It was just hiccups!" Zoha said quickly. "I ate too fast ... HIC!"

And before there were any more questions, she popped the spaceship in her pocket and ran.

2 A real, live, teeny tiny alien

With a small *ting-a-ling*, the spaceship door opened
and out stepped a real, live, teeny tiny alien. He was
no bigger than a baked bean. He was the colour of pea
soup. And his space suit was sparkling silver and white.

"So *you're* an alien," said the alien, peering at Zoha.
The creature raised one eyebrow thoughtfully.
"I've always wondered what aliens would look like.
I thought they would have more eyes."

"*I'm* not an alien," Zoha pointed out. "I live here. You've come from Space, which makes *you* the alien."

"True," said the alien, with a shrug. "Anyway, I'm Alan."

"And I'm Zoha," said Zoha.

"Sorry for landing in your lunch," said Alan.

"No problem," said Zoha. "It must have been tricky to touch down in that storm."

Alan spluttered with laughter. "That was no storm," he said. "That was the mother ship flying overhead. It launched my spaceship down to Earth with a catapult."

Zoha's eyes goggled.

"I've come from Planet Zeeble," Alan went on. "I work for a holiday company. All Zeeblings want to visit Earth. I have one week to discover all about your planet, so I can report back. Can you help?"

"I can't show you the whole planet in a week," said Zoha, "but I can show you the town where I live, if you like? It's called Smashing-on-Sea."

"Awesome," said the alien, whipping out a blue notebook. "I'll write everything down in here." He smiled broadly, showing his purple teeth.

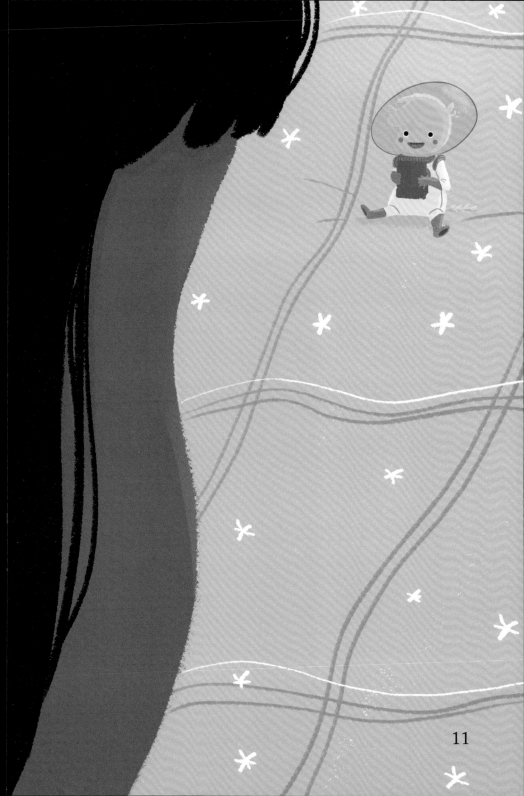

"How will you get back to the mother ship?" Zoha asked curiously. "Will the alien captain beam you up?"

Alan rolled his eyes. "Don't be silly," he said. "This isn't the future. Next Saturday at noon, the mother ship will lasso me as it whizzes past at a height of exactly one hundred metres. If it flies any lower, it'll crash."

This made Zoha very worried. "But Smashing-on-Sea is a small town with small buildings," she told the alien. "*Nothing* is one hundred metres tall."

"Don't worry," Alan said cheerily. "You'll think of something!"

3 The perfect way to travel

"Right," said Zoha. "How are we going to do this? You can't walk fast enough – and I don't want to tread on you. Can you fly?"

Alan rolled his eyes. "Do I look like a hot-air balloon?"

Zoha laughed. "I can carry you in my pocket?"

"No way," said Alan. "The view would be terrible. I'll ride on top of your head."

But Zoha didn't think it was a good idea to wear an alien like a hat. TV crews and scientists and super-nosy people would follow them *everywhere*. "Why don't you sit in my ear?" she said. "It'll be the perfect way to travel. You'll be warmer *and* I'll be able to hear you."

"That's *genius*." The tiny green alien stuck one hand in the air. "Give me a high six!"

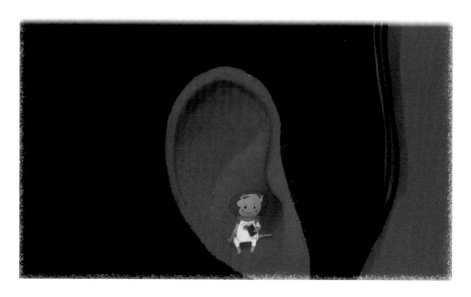

Alan climbed into Zoha's ear and said, "WHERE ARE
WE GOING FIRST?"

"Arrrrrrrrgh!" howled Zoha. He was louder than
a brass band. "Please can you whisper?"

"Oops," whispered Alan. "I didn't know that Earthling
ears were for hearing. I listen with my knees."

"Ah," said Zoha. "Well, we're going to the library.
It's full of – "

"Don't tell me! I want to guess!" interrupted the alien.
"It's full of spaghetti, right?"

"Not quite ..." said Zoha.

"Cake?" guessed Alan. "Chocolate? Daffodils? Formula One cars? I looked on the internet on the way here," he told Zoha proudly. "See how much I know about your planet already!" But after 237 guesses, he gave up.

"The library is full of *books*," Zoha whispered to him.

"Well, why didn't you say so?" said Alan.

"Let's go, Zoha!" said Dad.

At the Smashing-on-Sea library, Alan stared in wonder as Zoha explained how it worked.

"You borrow books for *nothing*?" he said. "Then you swap them for *more* books? You can read *as many books as you like*?"

Zoha nodded. "That's right." She had to agree. It *was* kind of amazing.

"STOP!" said Alan, as they passed one bookshelf. "What are *they*?"

"These books are filled with stories about Space and time travel and lots and lots of aliens," Zoha said. "It's the science fiction section." She held a book up to her ear so Alan could see.

"Wow!" breathed Alan. "I see now that I'm not the first alien to visit your planet. Others have been before me. That's why Earthlings know so much about us already!"

Alan didn't like
the shopping mall
so much.

"Pah!" he said.
"Shops are full of
shiny, useless things."

Luckily, he *did* like
riding in the lift.
"This is so clever,"
he whispered excitedly.
"It's a rocket that goes
up *and* down!

The seaside was a huge hit.

"Wow!" Alan murmured. "Look at that swishy sparkly stuff ... I know what it is! It's glitter! Earthlings use it to decorate spinning bow ties."

"Not quite ..." Zoha said. "It's the sea. You can paddle or swim *in* it. And you can sail or windsurf *on* it."

"I don't know what any of those things mean," said Alan, hopping up and down in Zoha's ear, "but I want to do them all!"

21

That night at the pizzeria, Alan hid under the edge of Zoha's plate. He helped himself to food when her parents weren't looking.

"What is *this*?" the alien demanded, his eyes gleaming as brightly as fairy lights. "It's so chewy! It's so stretchy! *I love it*!"

Zoha grinned. "It's a pizza," she whispered.

"I LOVE PIZZA," said Alan. "When they hear about pizza, every Zeebling on Planet Zeeble will want to visit Earth. Yummety-yum."

4 Wheeeeeeeeeeeeee!

Bzzzzt!

"What's that terrible noise?" howled Alan, sticking his head out of the spaceship. "It woke me up!"

"It's an alarm," said Zoha. "That's what it's supposed to do." She slid out of bed. "It's also Monday morning and it's time to get up for school."

"School? Hurray!" Alan did a cartwheel and a backflip. Then he sat down with an *oof*. "So, what's school?" he panted.

Zoha giggled. "It's a place where children learn things," she said.

"Perfect," said Alan. "Then I'll come with you. In five days, I'll be returning to Zeeble. School will help me find out EVERYTHING before then."

"What will we learn first?" said Alan, as the school door thwacked shut behind them.

When she was quite sure nobody was watching her, Zoha muttered, "Science."

"Great!" said Alan. "What's science?"

"It's all about how things work," said Zoha. "Maybe we'll learn how to send you one hundred metres into the air!"

But they learnt about the solar system instead.

"We should visit that pretty planet with the red spot," said Alan afterwards. "What was it called? Juniper!"

"*Jupiter* is millions of kilometres away," said Zoha. "It would take more than a year to get there."

"Wow!" said Alan. "Your spaceships are SO SLOW. Now I know why Earthlings never visit Zeeble."

That week, the teacher taught Alan and Zoha all sorts of wonderful things.

On Tuesday, they learnt about Earth's seasons. (Alan was disappointed that he wouldn't see snow in summer.)

On Wednesday, they learnt how people lived long ago. (Alan said next time he'd bring a time machine with him, so he could live long ago too.)

On Thursday, they learnt how to make a cake.
(Alan liked cake nearly as much as pizza.)

But they learnt nothing that could be used to send
an alien even ten metres into the air, never mind
one hundred metres. How *was* Alan going to reach
the mother ship and get back to Planet Zeeble?

On Friday afternoon after school, they went to the park.

"I wonder if we could swing you back to Space ...?" said Zoha, sailing backwards and forwards. "Maybe if I threw you into the air when I reached the very top – "

"I'm not listening!" squealed the alien. "This is ... *whee* ... so much ... *whee* ... FUN. *Wheeeeeeeeeeeeeee!*"

Zoha laughed and swung higher. "Look!" she said, pointing.

Across the park, skateboarders were doing tricks. One girl zoomed up a ramp and shot into the air.

"Earthlings can *fly*!" cried Alan. "My fellow Zeeblings are never going to believe *this*!"

When it was time to go home, they went to the bus stop.

"Is the bus coming now?" whispered Alan.

"No," Zoha whispered back.

"Now?" said Alan.

"Still no," Zoha replied.

"Now? Now would be good. Oh, I wish the bus was here now!" wailed Alan.

At that very moment, *three* buses arrived.

"My wish worked!" said Alan, dancing in Zoha's ear. "On your planet, I have a superpower! I can make things appear just by wishing for them!" He was silent for a moment, before adding, "I wonder if my superpower would work for pizza ...?"

5 Whizzing the little alien into the sky

By Friday evening, Alan's blue notebook was bursting with facts about Planet Earth. But Zoha still had no plan for whizzing the little alien into the sky.

Trampolines weren't bouncy enough.

Stilts weren't long enough.

And Zoha would be arrested if she fired him out of a cannon.

"*What are we going to do?*" she sighed.

"Relax!" said Alan. "You'll think of something."

"But I need to think of something *now*!" groaned Zoha.

"Look!" said Mum, pointing to the TV.

On the screen, there was the biggest
fairground wheel Zoha had ever seen.
At its centre, there was an enormous
neon eye. It turned slowly as
the wheel spun.

*"On Saturday, the famous eye-in-the-sky
will visit Smashing-on-Sea!"* announced
the presenter. *"Soar one hundred metres into
the air and enjoy the best view on
the planet!"*

Zoha felt like laughing and dancing and
doing a backflip, all at the same time.

"See? I knew you'd think of something,"
said Alan. "Now, how about some more
pizza to celebrate?"

6 The eye-in-the-sky

On Saturday morning, the weather was perfect for a spaceflight.

The eye-in-the-sky towered above Smashing-on-Sea. Cabins hung all around the huge wheel like ripe apples on a tree, shining in the sun.

Zoha shaded her eyes and squinted towards the top of the wheel. It was a very long way up. "Are you ready?" she whispered to Alan. The alien was strapped into his small, oval and very shiny spaceship, which was hidden inside Zoha's ear.

"I was born ready!" Alan replied.

"Let's go!" said Mum, climbing into the next cabin.

"I wonder if we'll be able to see our house ...?" murmured Dad, following her.

Zoha climbed in last. They were ready for lift-off.

The eye-in-the-sky turned slowly. The cabin climbed higher and higher. Zoha checked her watch. It was 11:59 a.m. In one minute, the mother ship would zoom past and lasso Alan on board. "Brilliant," she whispered. Everything had worked out perfectly.

THUNK.

The eye-in-the-sky stopped dead.

"Nooooooo!" groaned Zoha. The top of the wheel was still way above them. There was no way the fairground wheel could be fixed before noon. They would never make it in time and Alan would never get back to Zeeble.

It was a disaster!

The sky went dark. There were blinding flashes and
thundery rumbles. The wind blew harder than
a grandad puffing out candles. It was just like
a storm. But Zoha knew what was actually going on.
And it meant that they were too late ...

Then something wonderful happened. The blasts of air from the mother ship made the fairground wheel start moving again. The eye-in-the-sky turned … until Zoha's cabin was at the very top. She could hardly believe it. They were exactly one hundred metres high!

Zoha pulled the tiny spaceship from inside her ear and looked inside.

"We did it!" said Alan. He gave her a thumbs-up, with all four of his thumbs.

With a whispered "GOOD LUCK", Zoha launched
the spaceship into the air.

"Au revoir!" Alan called. "That means, 'until we see
each other again' – I read it in a book!"

A pink rope flew through the air and looped around
the spaceship. Then – with a mighty *whoosh* – Alan,
the spaceship *and* the mother ship were gone.

The sun came out and the eye-in-the-sky carried
on turning.

Zoha sighed with relief. Alan was on his way back to Planet Zeeble to tell everyone all about life on Earth. And if she wished very hard, maybe she *would* see him again. He might even bring a mother ship full of Space tourists with him.

Zoha smiled and gave a tiny wave. "Au revoir," she whispered.

Zeebling Travel presents ...

★ PLANET EARTH!

Our newest holiday destination.
It's out of this world!

If you're looking for a holiday that's a little bit different, why not travel to EARTH? This delightful blue and green planet is just a quick hop across the galaxy.

Visit an awesome LIBRARY, filled with books all about aliens. Earthlings know so much about us!

Ride in a LIFT. It's even better than a rocket – it goes down as well as up!

Watch Earthlings actually FLY.

Finally, no trip to Earth is complete without a chewy, stretchy PIZZA. It's the best meal in the universe!

Earth tours cost 500 Zeeblots and leave every Saturday at noon.

Ideas for reading

Written by Clare Dowdall, PhD
Lecturer and Primary Literacy Consultant

Reading objectives:
- recognise simple recurring literary language in stories and poetry
- make inferences on the basis of what is being said and done
- predict what might happen on the basis of what has been read so far

Spoken language objectives:
- give well-structured descriptions and explanations
- use spoken language to develop understanding through speculating, hypothesising, imagining and exploring ideas
- consider and evaluate different viewpoints

Curriculum links: Physical Education – throwing

Word count: 2487

Interest words: catapult, lasso, cannon, neon, destination

Resources: bean bags, hoops, pencils and large sheets of paper, whiteboards

Build a context for reading

- Look at the front cover and read the title of the story together.
- Ask children whether they like spaghetti and to describe how they eat it, building descriptive vocabulary, e.g. *I slurp it up; I twizzle it on my spoon.*
- Read the blurb together and ask children to suggest how the alien has got into Zoha's spaghetti, and to predict how he might get home again.

Understand and apply reading strategies

- Read Chapter 1 together, taking turns to read aloud. Encourage children to read with expression, enjoying the descriptive language, and engaging the listeners.
- Ask children to suggest what Zoha is thinking when she finds the tiny spaceship in her spaghetti. Collect children's ideas using thought bubbles on whiteboards, e.g. *How on earth did that get there? What is that doing in my delicious dinner?*